Reflections and Thoughts

Growth is the experiment in courage

By Sandra Pollock

SanRoo Publishing
is a Division of Inspiring You C.I.C.
ISBN 978-1-8384077-3-5

First published in Leicester, Great Britain in 2023
by
SanRoo Publishing

Copyright © Sandra Pollock OBE 2023

All Rights Reserved. The right of Sandra Pollock to be identified as the author of this work has been asserted by her in accordance with the Copyright, Designs and Patents Act 1988. No portion of this publication should be reproduced without prior permission stored in a retrieval system, or transmitted, in any form or by any means, electronic, mechanical, photocopying, recorded or otherwise without the prior permission in writing of the publisher, nor be otherwise circulated in any form of binding or cover other than that in which it is published and without similar condition including this condition being imposed on the subsequent purchase.

Proudly published in 2023 by SanRoo Publishing.
SanRoo Publishing is a division of Inspiring You CIC.
26 Bramble Way, Leicester, LE3 2GY, UK.
www.sanroopublishing.co.uk

ISBN 978-1-8384077-3-5

Contents

Reflections and Thoughts	2
Wisdom is Light	4
Wisdom	5
On the Sad and Gloomy days	9
For you - The women	10
Sister of the African Soil	11
Alter Ego	12
I've Grown	14
Salute The Black Sisters	16
Trading My Name	19
Broken Vow	20
My Barbadian Dialect	23
Glasses	24
Dressing Me	25
Girl Friend Circle – A New Man	26
Black is not darkness	28
Black	29
Let's do it, Let's talk	30
Not An Extension of Me	32
When Evil is Spoken	33
We have been here before	34
My Ancestors came to meet me	38
The Feeling of Creating	42
Lost	45
Summer Rains	46
Golden Solis	47
Ignored	48
Innocence	50
I'm Off On Holiday	53
The Mark I Made	54
A New Day	55

I Did Not Want To People Today	59
Listening to Spirit or the call of the Soul	61
The Call Of The Divine	62
The Painter	64
Listening To My Heart - Meditation	66
The Things I Love	69
This Is Not Going To Happen Often	71
Home Love	73
Lovers Walk	74
This List Gets Shorter	75
An Ode to Flapjack	76
And I Miss You	78
Life Is...	79
I'm A Poet	80
Poetic Place	81
About the Author	83

Reflections and Thoughts

Acknowledgements

Thanks goes to my wonderful daughter, Jerusha, who has been such a blessing and an inspiration to me in my life. She is my cheerleader and at times my guide and voice of reason.

To my husband, Mike, who is my supporter, challenger and friend.

To my best friend and writing buddy, Sonia Thompson, who graces me with her time regularly with repeated questions, and encouraging expectations of evidence that I have been paying attention to my creative gifts. Our weekly sessions have been a salve.

To Sammy Nour, whose passion for the spoken word has drawn me into opportunities, such as doing feature sets at Some-Antics and Shambala - along with my appearance to audiences in other places. I would not have considered this a possibility. Not forgetting my other Some-Antics friends, who have listened to my readings as I shared and tested many of these pieces to your willing ears.

And many other of my friends - too many to list here - who encouraged me to put this book together. I know it is long overdue.

May my musings and contemplations lift and inspire you, or at the very least make you think. With my blessing be all that you can be, no matter how different that might appear to others.

Thank you all.

Reflections and Thoughts

It's taken me a little longer than I had expected to put this book of thoughts together. I say thoughts, because poetry, like all other musings and creations, come from within and all starts with thought.

Like many in the artistic and creative arena, I sometimes have struggled with the issues of comparison and perfectionism. And yet the creative muse is persistent and for this I am really grateful.

In this book you will find thoughts and ideas that have run across my mind. Some may resonate, inspire and travel with you. For those that don't, just leave them behind.

I always find it amazing what can inspire me to create a poem, story, or just a piece of prose. This book carries no great message of contemplation. Rather, it is my opportunity to share a little of who I am in these words; there is no other cause.

Everyone dances to a tune, follows their own path and explores what life may bring - or at least they should. This is what I do when I sit down to write, draw, paint, or yield to any other creative spirit that I might feel. And doing this from my heart is my only personal cause.

Following traditions has been something I seem to be born to resist, so any who might find these writings outside of what might be considered the normal structure of doing creative writing things, be warned. Maybe it is not for you. But I hope you may find something to enjoy if you do take the time to read this book through.

Blessings and Light come from me to you.

Reflections and Thoughts

Wisdom is Light

Wisdom is a light.
Love, its sister shining bright.
The two giving sight.

Wisdom

Wisdom travels the Universe
Spreading herself like waves
Rippling through the air.

Running along the pathway of life
Ever ready to be picked up
By the enquiring mind
Of anyone, who need only whisper a call.

Wisdom is willing to share her gifts
To all who would just give her time.
Simple are her ways.
Like beautiful music is her voice.
Abundant are her messages and rewards.

Wisdom willingly shares.
If only we will adapt our ears
To her language of life.
So simple at times
Are the workings of universal laws.

Wisdom floats on, singing her call.
'Come gain my guidance, one and all.
Don't be too busy; don't be too crude;
Open your hearts to my life-giving food.'

There is no limit to what she will share,
From her open heart, good is there.
The price is time, quietness of heart and mind.
The practice built on self-belief.

Wisdom travels far but is always near.
Hers an ever open ear, listening for your call.
Her guidance immediately then appears,
Wanting nothing more than to be yours.

Sisters

Sandra Pollock OBE

On the Sad and Gloomy days

Sometimes I forget what I need,
To make sure that I am alright.
I spend my days and nights thinking that,
With just a bit more effort, I can take care of all others in my sight.
And though this is a fab thing we should all do,
It leads to nothing if you don't take care of you.

So when you're feeling low and under the weather.
When you can't seem to find a way to hold yourself together.
When there is no reason for the sense of dread, dark and damp.
When all the glimpses of sparkle have left your camp.

Remember that we all need a helping hand.
A little something extra to keep up our glam.
In my case, that is time sitting in front of my S.A.D. lamp.
To sort out the serotonin levels and reduce
The sense of foreboding and flat.

Whatever it is that you need for you,
To remain in balance and inwardly true,
Don't be ashamed to bring all else to a stop,
And grab what you need. A little top-up.

You are worth it, every slither and drop,
To bring you back on your sunshine spot.
Do all you need to do, to get back on top.
You're worth spending the time you need to be
Wonderfully you.

For you - The Women

You inspire, motivate, and delight.
Keep moving, spreading the glare of your light...
Forward,
Opening up distant unseen expanses of today and tomorrow.
Horizons now brighter, available to others' sight.

Only because a woman such as you
Refuses to be held,
Reducing
Your talents and dreams,
Limited by darkness.

But sees herself as the spear of pioneering gallant might.

To all women who fight equality's balancing fight.

Inspired by Carol Leeming MBE, Paulette Brown MBE, Amanda Leandro, Cllr Ashiedu Joel, Cllr Sue Hunter and other amazing black women from my local and family communities, past and present.

I'm sure you can add your own list of names to mine, too.

Sister of the African Soil

Welcome, Sister of the African Soil,
Mother of all humankind - girl and boy.
Come now into your own,
Fully realised to become the joy
of the world known.

Your time is here. Your time has come.
Your truth and worth has stood the test of time.
Your children stolen,
Your heritage denied for far too long.

The blackness of your beauty,
Which they all resisted, is found deep within
Their own mitochondrial birth.
To you belongs all upon this earth.

Welcome, Mother of African Soil.
Your children see you each generation,
Renewed over time.
Some resist the truth of earth's history.
But never as they try will they erase the depth
Of your eternal worth.

Alter Ego

"I am Princess Ebony De-Light.
I wear long, glorious, beautiful robes
Of luxurious gold, purple and white.

"I have a crown which changes size depending on the occasion.
Today it's the smaller crown, almost like a diadem -
Just to remind people of how glorious I am.
I live in a large, spacious palace,
With beautifully manicured gardens,
In a warm sunny climate.

"I have helpers who cater for my every need.
Whilst I spend my time in meditation, and
Giving guidance and advice to those in need, who come to me."

We should all imagine an alter ego.
It's a fanciful, empowering exercise that makes us smile.
We should all hold wistful dreams in our heads,
Where no one else can see - there to withdraw and hide.

We should all have an alter ego
That takes us to our own land of dreams,
And helps us escape from difficult things
Just for long enough
To return us with strength to fight on.

We should all have an alter ego.
One that when people hear about it they would cry,
'You're crazy to think such things.'

We should all have an alter ego,
For going to that place, reminds us of how children dream.

My favourite writing exercise:
One of the exercises I encourage our delegates to do in the Creative Writing sessions that Sonia Thompson and I run.
The aim is to create a space where we fuel our dreams and write about who we would dream to be: our alter-ego.
I have found this to be a most expansive exercise and takes people (men and women) into a place where their dreams and visions of themselves expand, allowing them to step into the freedom of creativity, self belief and self value.
Give it a try.

I've Grown

I've grown.
I've grown as a woman.
I've learnt to appreciate my blackness,
My history, my culture, my womanness -
My unique experiences.

I've grown
in my expansion of network and friends.
I've grown in knowledge. I've become more me.
I've collaborated. I've listened. I've laughed. I've cried.
I've learnt to become more free with me.

I've journeyed across the world through the eyes and works
of sisters I didn't know I had.
I've grown stronger, more open as the world has become smaller,
Through the impact that Covid-19 had.

I've changed forever and now cannot go back.
This programme has enable me to do all that, and more.
So Life, I thank you for that.
I've grown.

Reflections and Thoughts

Most of us will remember the impact that Covid-19 has had. Far too many will recall its negative impact. But there have been beneficial things too, even if it is just the recognition that we are social beings that need social and physical contact. Let's not forget, in our return to the busyness, of what was before that.

During the Covid-19 pandemic, my friend, Sonia Thompson, and I ran a creative writing programme for women of African-Caribbean and Asian heritage called 'Create Together'. The programme was run online, but most of the women were based in Leicester - the city given the most periods of lockdown in the UK. The programme gave support to women, to help them deal with their mental and emotional stress. It was transformational to our participants and to me. You will not be surprised to note that creative writing was one of the activities included in the programme. The anthology, 'Create Together: Our Voices, Our Hands, Our Lives' came from this programme, and can be purchased from SanRoo Publishing or good bookstores.

Salute The Black Sisters

Here we are looking into the future.
Eyes bright, mind alert, hope ignited.

Here we stand shoulder to shoulder.
In this moment of time.
A month's recognition, for centuries of untold labour and burden.

Still, courage engaged. Confidence emboldened
By the hope that our tomorrow will be better,
Starting today.

Every day, Equality cries, "Celebrate our sisters."
"Those matriarchs of movements, long ignored and forgotten. Overwritten."
"Salute our sisters, who stand today in the gateway of the almost forgotten."

How will *our* history be written?
It is being written now,
Within the pen of decision-making held in your hands.

To empower a better future, we must recognise where we are today,
And what actions and inactions we all share that brought us here.

No great platitudes on whimsical soliloquy
can bring the future that makes us all free.

If woman - any woman, the black woman - is not free to be,
Then none are free to be.
Don't we all come from she?
Mother,
Bearer of all who is humankind,
Humanity?

Salute the brave black sisters,
who, while still bearing children to slavery,
Blows, rejections, abuse, and poverty,
Forge through. Using her wits and intelligence. Taking a stand.
Holding the right of freedom gripped
So tightly in her hands that her veins are made to bleed -
Along with her back, her mental health, her physical health, and her well-being.

Each day she still feels the whip that keeps her down.
Opportunities withheld.
Promotions passed over.
Ideas stolen. Servitude enshackled.
'C' suite roles blocked and benefits forbidden.

Yet, hear her cry,
In streets, in homes, in market places, in offices, and businesses,
In creative and innovation arenas,
Creating her own spaces to shine.

History will forever tell her story of resistance, resilience,
Emboldened, and empowered with a life source that can never be put out.
It has and will travel through each generation.
Passed down through the DNA.
In every age she is there.

This future we seek, and hear calling to us,
Is her voice.
A song she forever sings. The voice of freedom.
True freedom that recognises her humanity -
Black people's humanity.
Her right to be, in each place, at each table, at each level,
In each space and time.
Because her gift is given just as those held by any other,

Sandra Pollock OBE

To powerfully declare truth and justice to all humankind.

She is, and will always be the voice of wisdom.
She is made of a black skin that shines.
Salute the black sister with more than just words,
But with value, respect, recognition, support, opportunity, and equal pay.

Amend the past by how you treat her today.

Salute my black sisters.

Trading My Name

Walked to the counter, ordered coffee.
"Your name?" - this is what she wanted to know from me.
Names given just for coffee.
What do you think this means?

She wrote it on a cup, turned her back and moved on.
Away from me.
Standing in line, waiting my turn for coffee to be made.
I can see all the actions, preparation, ingredients all in blend.

I stand there and pretend,
That waiting is part of us becoming friends.
Three minutes wait.

My name I hear.
I raise my eyes to follow the sound.
The actions don't support
What I think calling my name should surround.
Emptiness is all that was followed through.

Giving you my name
Did not create the connection
Such a personal gift should do.

Cold, expressionless impressions are all that I get.
And I gave so much.
I gave my name for a coffee cup.

Broken Vow

I tried not to end your life as you made your web in the corner.
Advising you once or twice your choice might bring you danger.
The steam rose as I removed my clothes and stepped behind the curtain.
I hoped that you would stay enclosed within your self-made container.
But out you came and ran across the ceiling above me.

I knew exactly what you'd do, thinking I'd be good for dinner.
I warned you then again and again not to become a swinger.
My gentle voice made you believe that harm would be a stranger.
So down you dropped and out I jumped throwing water everywhere.

The floor now soaked, curses evoked, still tenderness for you I engendered.
I spattered water at you to change your course but fiercely you competed.
Until a flood washed you from the silken thread above my head,
Knocking you against the wall, carrying you down beneath.

Your small and fragile body lay now broken at my feet.
I'd made a vow to harm no creature, insect or bird encountered.
To share the space together and to live in respectful unity.
But I will defend my right to life from even a little spider.
For one so small you made a call and showed a bellicose nature.
And thus, my vow not to harm your kind was reluctantly broken and in tatters.

Ocean Depths

Sandra Pollock OBE

My Barbadian Dialect

Although I've written poems and songs since I was a child, it has taken me many years to appreciate much of my own Barbadian culture, which has included our beautiful melodic dialect.

Over the past ten years or so I've reclaimed this for myself by writing many of my poems in the Barbadian dialect. It is much more effective when spoken, but it is my joy to share some of these with you.

I have found many of the thoughts and reflections that deal with racism, gender and similar equality issues come to me within the dialect that formed my early years. Clearly this is a place where I find comfort and self expression.

I am certainly by far not the first person to write in our cultural tongue. But each person ventures into a discovery of their own, and this, when it happens, deserves a noted celebration.

These poems deal with issues of deep emotion, that some might find it surprising for me to share them here or at all. But courage is the foundation of voice.

In my business life I deal with these topics of inequality in a more managed way. My personal view is that we are all one - one human race. It is fear, and the decisions of some to believe differently, that causes us to distribute such pain to each other.

However, even knowing this and believing as I do has not shielded me from the feelings, the pain and disappointment, of being treated as less than human at times, in the day-to-day of living in this human space.

Glasses

De odder day I loas my glasses.
I couldn't fine dem anywhere.
Dem not in de baatroom, de kitchen, de bedroom.
No matter where I look,
I couldn't fine dem.

It mek me tink bout mobile phones.
At least when I caan't fine my phone,
I can call it.
When I hear it ring, I know jus where it is.
But I caan do dat wid a pair of specs.

Dem does sit round,
Quietly waiting to be discovered.
Dem can't shout, raise an arm and wave at me.
Even if daay could,
It might be a little hard to see.

Somebody could mek nuff money,
Creating someting dat could fine my glasses fuh me.
But in de meantime,
I off to try and put my hands on glasses pair, number t'ree.

Dressing Me

I went out to de shops today,
Trying to fine someting to wear.
You'll be surprise to know,
I couldn't fine a ting.
No sah, not a ting to fit in.

Dem doan mek clothes fah people like me,
Who doan look like a walking tree.
My curves and bumps, dem just doan seem to see.
De trousers and skirts, not mek fah a girl like me.

When it fit de top,
Dee bottom part can't swing.
When it fit de front,
Dee back caan closen in.

I nearly come out tonight
In a plastic bag.
'Cause dat was all it seem
I hadn't tried.

My body appears to be a dichotomy,
To de fashion houses on de high street.
A complete glorious puzzle, yah see.

So, when dem decide to dress a real woman -
And dat gorgeousness does come in ever size -
I'll be happy to go back to de high street again.
And my distress at fining clothes,
Will have come to an end.

Girl Friend Circle – A New Man

Hey, you going out wid he?
He look like he only about t'ree.
Who he modda? Who he fadda be?
My daughter might know he sister or brodda.
Let me ask and see.

He does work? He got a job?
You not frighten somebody tek you fa he modda?
Girl, I would tink again, if I was you.
Maybe he just taking you for a fool.

You say he really nice and kind.
Chyle I tink you might be loosing you mind.
I tink we need to call a meeting of de girls to discuss all ah dis.
You caan mek a decision like dis on you own.
Who gon sort out tings for you if anyting go wrong?
We, you girl friends, got to check he out.
We need to fine out what he is all about – what is lie and what is tru.

You alright talking 'bout he good in bed.
We need to check out what going on in he head.
I know he check by you, but dat not good enough.
We, you friends, got to mek he life tough.
He need to understand you life important to us
And dere ain't no space for no foo foo man.

He got to be able to stand up tough.
Six month probation should be nuff.
Yes, let we put in time and contemplation.
His approval is what in question.

He need to know that you got people who care 'bout you, ya hear?
Dis is a whole girl-friend-family, t'be clear.
Girl friends dat don't get push aside just because a man decide to swing by.
Or even if he choose to stay.

So bring he round dis Friday night.
Nice food and lots of questions are in sight.

In many communities, especially my own, a trusted group of girlfriends is an important part of a woman's life. This group of friends may not be big, but it is powerful and influential. It is near impossible for an individual member to do anything without it being discussed by the group. It's like having sisters, and everything is up for discussion. Everything.

Starting a relationship with a new man can become one of the juiciest parts of discussion. The man has to get the approval of the friend-group. This does not mean that the woman in question cannot decide for herself, but her friends will have a whole heap of questions which they will expect to find answers to. There will be an initial meeting where the guy will have to face questions along with observation and scrutiny of everything he does.

Through this poem I share in a fun way a conversation that might take place between girlfriends, the experience and questioning the girl might go through herself as she talks with her friends about her new boo.

Black is not darkness

Black is not darkness.
Darkness is absence of light.
Black makes heat from light.

Black

Did you not realise that everything starts with black?
The radiant brightness of light cannot be seen
Without the blackness of night?

Black
Did you not realise that white,
Needs the contrast and deepness of black,
Before it can be recognised to sight?

Black is the foundation of all,
The place everything comes from,
And to where it all returns.

Black is what makes us see the glory of the stars.
The reflection of the sun, worlds like Jupiter and Mars.
Black draws attention to all.

Is a black hole not so mysterious a sight,
As to keep astronomers guessing,
What could be so powerful as to swallow light?

Are these mysterious objects the beginning or the end?
The start of life, foe, or friend?

Black is beautiful, I was always taught as a child.
Powerful and strong, divine, full of pride.
To be able to take such ill treatment, endure such wrong,
Yet still hold up the placard that sings justice's song.

Black, I am proud to be...
I am Black...
I will hold justice and right strong, and sing the song of nights.
Black.

Let's do it, Let's talk

Let's do it,
Let's talk about... hair,
Black hair, my hair.
It seems to me that it's not mine at all,
The frequency with which your hands reach out
to touch it, and all.
The way your fingers twist around the curls
And wrap and feel the way it swirls.

Let's do it,
Let's talk about... space,
Personal space - my personal space.
The way you don't recognise it at all,
The boundaries you break repeatedly, stepping in close,
Not realising when you do reach out and grab my hair,
That you forcibly intrude, just there about.

Yes, let's do it,
Let's talk about... assault.
The number I experience each day is an interesting thought.
The way you assault me when you fail to ask and wait.
You touch my hair like I'm not there.
It's not a complement for me, I swear.

Let's do it,
Let's talk about... the... objectification.
This degradation that leads me to despair.
When you don't see me as human,
But just an object to be touched, explored, prodded and pulled.
And, if I retaliate, I'm the one that's no good.

Yes, let's do it,
Let's talk about... feelings.
My feeling, because I have them too.
You never imagining that I could feel threatened, uncomfortable,
Used or abused,
By your ignorance and disrespect, the white privilege you choose.
Sooo wrapped up in your obsessive desire to touch my hair, feel my skin, craw into my bed.
You just do the things you feel you have the right to do,
With no regard or thought for the person you just look through.

Come on then, let's do it now, let's talk
About the woman I am.
The creation that, just like you, is a human...
Being,
A gift of life.
Trying to exist without trouble or strive.
I am someone's daughter, sister, friend or spouse.
Here with the potential of a full life, to live out.

Come now, let's talk about it,
How your unconscious biases impact on
The choices of my black life,
But let's also note that change is a-foot.
And growing in strength everywhere you look.
With strength welling up in her heart with cries of "no more!
"Time to Stop."

Let's do it... Let's talk... about Truth.

Not An Extension of Me

It may not look like it,
But it's a part of me.
Like the nails of my fingers
The flair of my nostrils.
It's all me.

No-one would ever think they could just play
With someone else's toes,
Just reach for a person's feet.
You'd think that was crazy,
An insult, objectionable and far from discreet,
An intrusion of personal space, so to speak.

But with black hair there's no such retreat.
Somehow people don't seem to see or think.
The deep-curled softness on top of my head,
Is as much a part of me,
As the lips on my face,
And the voice I use to speak.

Someone fluffing my hair or patting my head,
Is as cringe-worthy as lying in a coffin with someone dead.
Even that would be considered a personal assault, I suppose.

The first person charged with touching someone's hair
Without consent would prove such a delightful treat.
And may just help you to realise - get the message I speak,
That my hair is not an unattached heap.
It's part of my person, whatever the style.
Keep your hands out of my hair,
And we'll both continue to smile.

When Evil is Spoken

Do not be silent when wrong is done.
When evil is spoken as truth or fun.
Do not let these things be done,
Without your voice being heard
Amongst those who say "no, that is not good."
Do not stand by and allow justice to be overrun.

When at times you appear to be the only one
Standing for what is right and true.
Be the one that says out loud,
"No, good and right should be done."

When tyranny is pushed as of benefit to all,
By those who have been given our trust by the vote,
To guide the youth, look after the old and feed the poor.
When those who are led by greed and darkened hearts rule,
Let not your voice be silent and still.
We are not fools.
Let not your choice or spirit be overruled.

When evil is spoken and paraded as good.
Let not your knowledge of right be trodden underfoot.
Courage and justice stand with the good.

We have been here before

You think we've never been here before, but
Yes, we've travelled this path I'm sure.
Queen Charlotte ruled Briton and Ireland from shore to shore.

Queen's Lodge at Windsor was her abode,
With King George III and the fifteen children shared.
You think we've never been here before.

These days ignoring the past is such a bore,
Pretending the line is white European and nothing more.
Queen Charlotte ruled Briton and Ireland from shore to shore.

Now just as Prince Harry has chosen a woman he adores,
And her ancestry is joint black and white.
You think we've never been here before.

In times when marriage choices are made on love,
And not on union of country, state or political debate.
Queen Charlotte ruled Briton and Ireland from shore to shore.

We wish them happiness, joy and so much more.
Bringing unity to the hearts of people who look on.
You think we've never been here before, but
Queen Charlotte ruled Briton and Ireland from shore to shore.

The call to return...

Sandra Pollock OBE

A visit to South Africa

A few years ago, I had the opportunity to go to South Africa. Johannesburg to be precise. It was a business trip, a successful one. My colleagues and I worked with a department of the South African government, providing Leadership Coaching support.

Visiting Johannesburg was very revealing. The contrast of poverty and wealth existing immediately next to each other... But that is another story for another day. What I want to share was an experience that took place for me long before I came to note those disparities.

My heritage is African, via Barbados in the Caribbean. The knowledge of my African heritage has never been lost on me, but I had never really thought I would visit the African continent. It had long been on the list of things I wished to do, and visiting again still is now. There is so much of that massive continent to explore and discover.

I am sure if you travelled by plane to a hot country, you've felt the weight of the hot breeze on your face. I had many times before. This time, however, it was something far more. It was something far different, and something I will never forget. This experience was so profound, personal and lasting, that it has taken me years to be able to put words to it...

My Ancestors came to meet me

My Ancestors came to meet me.
Greetings strong, welcoming, and proud,
That the offspring of African soil
Returned home and could be found.

My Ancestors came to meet me,
Rushing forward through the skies,
Pressing spirit with soul blessings,
Pushing deep into my bones again to abide.

Yes, my Ancestors came to meet me,
Long before my feet touched the soil
Of African continent brown.
Foundational land of so much toil.

My Ancestors came to meet me.
I left them generations upon generations ago.
Now they advanced forward dancing,
Stamping bare feet against the ground.

My Ancestors came to meet me,
If Spirit's tears could be felt,
Then six hundred years of weeping,
To see the child once stolen
Find her way back home emboldened.

My Ancestors came to meet me,
Welcoming me home again.
When once I was lost and broken,
Now I find belonging, place, home and hope.

Yes, my Ancestors came to meet me,
They could not wait until the steps I did alight,
But at the door of the plane as I stood,
Their breath of love was clear delight.

My Ancestors came to meet me,
And though the language I could not speak,
The powerful message flooded
My mind, heart and spirit deep.
Beating out the darkness from my soul,
Returning it to the light.

Yes, my Ancestors came to meet me.
Now what delight my life engages.
I am who I know myself to be.
And though the centuries have forged deep
And searing distances,
There can no greater power be,
Than the love of my Ancestors for me.

To The Universe we all belong

Reflections and Thoughts

The Feeling of Creating

I love the feeling of creating.
It is beautiful and open, expansive and moving.
It is curious, nosy, inquisitive, and wants to go.

It is unafraid to open a new door.
Break things down and throw them onto the floor
Just to see what might happen.
Or to answer the question, 'what more?'

It is cleansing, therapeutic prayer.
Yet in all this, not demanding of anything other than your time.
You can open your hands and let the music go,
Or you can give it care, focus and space to allow it to grow.

I love creating,
It's the release of the Divine Creator within me.
The exhilaration of letting myself go free.

Melancholy

Sandra Pollock OBE

Lost

It's lost, that self assurance I used to have.
It's gone, the power of knowing, which was never bad.
I don't know how I lost it.

Maybe I need to shout this out.
Call it out, loud enough for it to hear,
To draw it back, keep it near and circling about.

Or should I just write it down -
This truth of how I feel -
In the hope that doing this will help me to heal?

There is no shame in being real.
Connecting with emotions of sadness or joy
All that makes you feel... life!
These things you should employ.

And change is a part of life, I know,
Even though... it disorientates you...
Causing inner chaos and strife.
Its power can overtake you.

Loss is the gain of something new.
The power of a different experience,
Unpleasant at times but true.
Another part of what makes you... you.

I'll find me again,
Renewed, uplifted, inspired, and gifted too.
And then the lost will be found, and I...
I will be brand-new.

Summer Rains

Summer Rains.
Warm and gentle.
Lightly touching on the ground.

Summer Rains.
Warm and gentle.
Recognisable, when we hear its sound.

Summer Rains.
Warm and gentle,
To past memories, through it, we are bound.

Summer Rains.
Warm and gentle.
Lovers arms encase me with that sound.

Summer Rains.
Warm and gentle.
It comes again and makes my soul sing.

Summer Rains.
Warm and gentle
A gift from mother nature I hold forever within.

Golden Solis

Did you say you wanted a golden one?
A dream child that reflects the sun.
Hair bright and eyes of light.
Beauty to compare to none?
Well here you are, but note with this,
One price is to be paid with each annual drift.
Not a full life, maybe half of one,
To keep away the grey in which this mission begun.

Did you say you wanted just one?
So the villagers see you as blessed and begun?
As fortunate, one the gods have not forgotten?
Well here you have one made of two halves.
Whose light and darkness both have needs to be met.
Recompense to balance the sound introspection.

Did you say while deep in despair?
You'd give all you have for this one here?
Maybe the choice you made when in so deep
Withheld secrets you need to keep.
Did you say you wanted a single yellow?
Here now, Solis has given you its best.
But are you really now up to the test?

Did you say you wanted a golden one?
A dream child that reflects the sun.
Holding this child in your arms,
Your labours have begun.

Ignored

I followed you around like a little sheep, walking two steps behind.
Just to bow at your feet, admiring you on my own and deep within
my mind.
You didn't see me hold on to the rope that kept me near you.

I copied all you did, I learned to smoke.
Lighting cigarettes and marijuana too.
I nearly choked, it was so dope, but then I didn't mind.
You never saw how much of you I'd take.
Working to do all I could to imitate.

But you left me behind, ignored like the skittish child I was -
No confidence in myself, little self-worth.
You did not see me in all my troubled state.
To you I was just a joke to make.

I wanted to be just like you; I thought you had arrived
Full of determination, never misunderstood.
You seemed to have it all there, where you stood.
Only now looking back I realise that in the shield,
With which you covered yourself,
You too held much emptiness inside.

I think of you occasionally and wonder where you are,
What has happened in your life and if you wear your scars
with pride.
The marks we all bear growing through our years
To become the person we believe it would be fun to be.
Have your choices brought you all the things you wished your life to be?

I wonder if you stumbled across my name,
On some social media trek.
What would you think this person you've read about had made of themselves...
Anything worthwhile yet?
Would you still think I was someone to forget?
Would you even recognise the life that once so clung to yours?
Or would you say in retrospect, "She's no-one to forget"?
"No, this girl is someone who should not be ignored."

Reflecting on my teenage years when I hung ground a girl a few years older than me. I do wonder where she is now.

Innocence

I love the ignorance of innocence.
The lack of knowing what others think is right.
The restrictions of so-called proven experience,
That somehow inhibits your movement and foresight.

Not knowing what has gone before,
What expected outcomes should appear.
Not being channeled down an already travelled path
With results ready given and clear.

I love the freedom of just going ahead,
And acting on dream-power's glorious vision,
Not hampered by fear's restrictions,
Or negative voices ringing in your ear.

With your eyes open wide and focused,
Only on the soon to be realised, inspired creation.
That's the power that pulls you forward,
To bring you into the taste of your heart's heaven.

But when we've become seasoned with much rejection,
Disappointment, and far too many voiced introspections.
Playing it safe within the lines can appear a safer haven.

And when this happens you lose another piece of heart freedom:
The creative essence that is you -
Broken off by the words of another,
Attempting to reform themselves by living through you.

I love the ignorance of innocence;
Untethered by experience's song.
Rushing headlong through the gates.
Excited to know all that awaits before too long.

I love the innocence that optimism frames,
Across the minds of the eager-hearted.
Who know no bounds or limitations,
And fail to see the possible complications.

But gleefully presses on to create the length
And breadth of all that might be possible.
Holding a vision of life and joy within the spark,
That rings out from deep within the joyousness of innocence's heart.

I miss the innocence once fostered deep within my soul.
I now try so hard to regain its reconnection.
I seek the purity of ignorance of old.
The gift that unknowing bestows.

Sandra Pollock OBE

Going down to the Sea

I'm Off On Holiday

Okay, a holiday is brewing.
I can feel it in my bones.
It may just have to be a few days,
But that's okay, that's just how things go.

I may have to imagine distant oceans and
My toes pushing down into the sand.
Hey, that's the type of things dreams are made of.
It's those pictures that draw a new reality in.

So, yes, a holiday is brewing.
I can feel it in my bones.
For now though, I'm searching the internet for images,
To create that experience I'll never forget.

I can walk along this beautiful beach.
I can get my feet wet.
I can wear a pretty swimsuit and forget about a hairnet.

The brain does not differentiate,
The difference between the real
And the ideas in my head.

So, I'm off to visit Barbados and sit in the sun.
My back garden can become
Anywhere I can dream.
I'm having fun.

The Mark I Made

There's a mark on my thigh.
I got it in my youth,
Trying to take a simple crease,
Out of a pleat in my school skirt.

The iron was not very forgiving on that date
To a girl who didn't think things through.
My skin was, I thought, protected
By the layers of the material,
But the heat made it's way through.

The mark is still there,
In the shape of a Q,
A Q... To remind me not to forget,
That who I am is no accident or mistake,
But one created by Divine design.

Q is the starting letter
Of many things I like best, like...
Quickies, Quilts, Questioning, and Quest.
Quiet, Quartz and Queen.

Quintessentially...
My mark is that of an African Queen.
Eternally branded...Q.

A New Day

The morning greets me with a smile,
Arms opened wide,
Bearing gifts with pride,
"A full new day created for you," she cries.

Skipping on ahead,
Joyfully riding the ocean tide.
Come follow, don't stay inside,
In the gloom of a frustrated mind.

Jump on the breeze,
Let's take a ride.
Let me show you
Where hope and possibilities reside.

I take her hand and as I look ahead.
I feel my insides rise,
And forever spread before my mind's eyes
Is the promised land where
My dreams and hopes abide.

Emotional Entanglement

Reflections and Thoughts

The challenges of the empathetic soul

I love people, and I am energised by sharing my thoughts with others and hearing their returning views. Yet, even then, there are times when am unable to handle the torrent of emotional energy I pick up from the people around me...

My open empathetic spirit can sometimes be too open to the world of emotional tides...

I Did Not Want To People Today

I did not want to people today.
I just wanted to stay in my bed and while the hours away.
Yesterday I thought it might be a good idea to go shopping tomorrow.
But when tomorrow arrived and presented itself as today, all ideas of peopling vanished into thin air.

I do not want to people today.
It seems so much easier staying under the covers and letting my thoughts stray.
I know I need to buy some new shoes; my sneakers are giving me the blues.
But that would mean fighting through the crowds,
Dealing with all of the emotional energies, thoughts and struggles packed into the small space of the shopping mall.

No, I don't want to people today.
But I love people, I always say.
I want to help them as much as I can,
Taking care of their hurt emotions, and undecided thoughts and plans.
Holding space for them until they can see the light that's already shining within them: life's eternal degree.

But I can't people again today.
My inner light is in need of replenishing and repair.
I am exhausted, requiring my own quiet space
For peace, harmony, inspiration, love and grace.

I do not want to people today.
Today is time for me to connect with the Infinite Creator within.

My wish is not to people today.
It's not about you in any way.
It is a reminder to me that I've spent my last dime of energy.
Too much giving out. Too little balance at play.

I am still, mind quiet,
Enveloped outside of space and time.
Learning to keep the noise out -
Noise of the physical world around and about.
I may remain here, still and quiet, in my mind.
Enjoying the beauty of spirit silence.
Feeding my existence with Light and Love.

No, my new shoes will have to wait.
I am not going to people today.

Listening to Spirit or the call of the Soul

Some would say that all of our creativity is a result of listening to the call of Spirit.

We know there is a time when we're in the right vibration of mind and spirit, where we connect to a flow. That energy or feeling that everything seems to move, gathering towards you every thing you need: whether writing, painting, or creating a song or a sculpture of some kind.

Our effects appear easy, effortless and divine. If only we could find a way to make this happen all the time...

The Call Of The Divine

Maybe that loneliness I feel
Is you calling to me.
To come and spend time and be free.
In our quiet place within, for you and me.

I'd never thought of that before,
That you could need me too,
Resting at your open door.
How real, this truth now new.

To learn how loneliness could feel,
Without first having to know
The sense of separation,
The opposite of wanting to let go.

Now I want to hold in the consciousness of
My heart and mind, the knowing
That when the deep longing comes,
That yearning within me I feel.

It is that difference between space and time.
Not the sense of separation but an open door to find.
It may just be you calling to me once more,
For meditation and quiet connection to be sure.

Could be the middle of the day or
In the hastening shadows of night.
These are only gifts of peace, harmony, answered
Questions that float to me from Spirit to my mind.

Now I know this is your call to release
The stressful things of daily life,
And our place to find a more peaceful way,
A different vibrational soul-food on which to dine.

I must remember to take this time to connect with you.
It is always so sublime.

The Painter

The Painter was up this morning,
Well before the crack of dawn.
Choosing colours to spread across
The sky on this special morn.

What is it that makes this day special?
Why choose a new pallet today
To throw out ahead of the sun, across the sky,
And interrupt its way?

Her question formed a wrinkled line
That marked her gentle brow.
Childlike curiosity filled the eyes
Looking to the clouds up high.

"This day has never been before,"
The Painter smiled a reply.
"And will never come again.
Just like those clouds passing by."

He kissed her forehead as he spun,
Throwing the colours to the sky.
Then in response the clouds change,
A burst of yellow, orange and pink filled her eyes.

The beauty of the moment caused her heart to stop and sing.
Paint-dipped cotton streaks burst with passion across the eager sky.
A grin from her, a wink she catches from the Painter's eye.

Each day must be resplendent,
Marking history's eternal pride.
Like snowflakes each day is different,
And must make that statement as it travels by.

When you have grown and seen many dawns,
Soon the wonder you will ignore.
Forgetting that each day is a new and open door.
You may paint the colours of your life.
Some days bright and others with gloom,
But no one day is ever anything but brand new.

Don't ruin the new day with colours of days past.
Don't dull down what is bright and new.
Let each morning's light burst across the sky,
An original, just like you.

Choose your pallet of colours each morn.
Let them reflect what you wish the day to do.
Throw out your wishes, your thoughts, your goals.
The dreams of happiness, success and joy you wish to draw to you.

Then like the Painter of the dawn,
Choose your pallet anew.
Paint your intentions for each day.
Throw them out across the sky and
You will draw good things to you.

Listening To My Heart - Meditation

I am still, calm and relaxed.
Body quiet, muscles still,
Excessive energies reduced.
Shoulders rested, limbs floppy,
Inner ears open and listening
To the words and leadings of my heart.

I am still, mind quiet.
Words floating across like clouds.
Visible but fleeting, leaving no marks where they once drew.
Whether stressful or good.
Just clouds travelling through.

I am still, mind quiet, focused inward to the deep.
Into the facets of Spirit where I want my heart to seek.
Far beyond the busyness of every day.
Trailing the aeons of time.
I am beyond that now.
To the quietness of my mind,
That speaks to my soul.

I am still, mind quiet.
Not seeing outside, but worlds deep within,
Far beyond where words can begin...
To explain the place of supreme infinite,
The super consciousness of mind,
The source that formed my spirit being's beginning,
Where home is the place I find.

I am still, listening to the words of my heart,
Where reactions come more quickly than the brain can carry a start.
Where truth, my truth, can eternally be found.
The place I long to stay for as long as I possibly can.

Love seeps through...

Sandra Pollock OBE

The Things I Love

Spring days -
Uplifting and forward looking,
Telling me life will be okay.

The sight of new buds of life sprouting
From the tips of old tree branches.

The sound of the sea -
Waves rolling over the ancient sands,
Like lovers greeting each other with
A passionate roar as they embrace.

The way that love itself
Can bring the most powerful to their knees.

The manipulation of words onto the page,
Combined so well they resonate
Through the ages to tell
Of mischief or peace.

The sounds of laughter and noisy chatter
When friends meet or gather.

My father's deep and heavy voice,
Still with an accent that years in this country
Could never break.

The words, "Hi Mum,"
That burst through any fog, any focus of my mind,
To take precedence over all space and time,
My attention to bind.

Sandra Pollock OBE

The feeling of small, fluffy, four-legged
Furry things, brushing against my feet.
With cries of "pay me attention.
I want something to eat!"

The fact that the list of the things I love
Will take a lifetime and beyond to complete.

This Is Not Going To Happen Often

This is not going to happen often.
Just whenever I feel the need
To stretch out my hand and find you there,
Like grass growing between the weeds.

Don't get used to these feelings,
I must keep moving on,
Forward and restless, like the flow of water strong,
Rolling down the mountainside, picking up speed as I go.
This will not happen often, just so you know.

Separation is what I think I need.
Though loneliness drives me to the door,
Out into the street only to find you,
To satisfy this hunger that starts gnawing
In the palms of my hands,
Ever needing to touch you.

Stroke your face, then your brow
As we fall onto the floor.
This is not going to be often.
Ignore the cries and groans that call for more.
Only a part-time thing, you know,
That I can't seem to leave behind for long.
You begin to invade my dreams. Your smell is so strong.

This is not going to happen often.
This intermittent longing brings me around full-circle.
Stop this magic you must be weaving.
Set me free, I implore.

This is not going to happen often,
To see your eyes yearning and strong.
Although I tell you again and again as we rise
This is not going to be often,
Do not ask for more in disguise.

Who says love, if this is what this is,
Must be permanent and concreted?
That would spoil the music and the song.
And this melodic piece should never drag on, to make it weak.
So just be warned, don't ask for more.

This is not going to happen often,
I say again as I leave your door.

Home Love

We always desired a home of our own,
One with a garden in which we can roam.
With upstairs and downstairs, kitchen and bath.
With a place to be separate, a little front path.

Where flowers grow yearly without much demand.
We can nourish them daily with our gentle hands.
Somewhere we can enter and close the door,
Knowing we're happily home and secure.

Where warm colours and soft furnishings surround.
The smell of cakes baking, and conversation resound.
A life to share our happiness there.
The place where love grows, my life built with you.

Home is the physical touches we create,
When chances pass by or stop at our gate.
In our deepest part is where the magic starts.
Home is created when love lives in the heart.

Lovers Walk

We ventured out into the evening light.
The moon gazed out from behind the clouds.
The stars shared our hearts, shining bright.

The path along the hillside heights
Enticed us to dream of future lives.
We ventured out into the evening light.

Declaring beyond life's limited plight,
Our love will last forever and a night.
The stars shared our hearts, shining bright.

As flesh touched flesh in amorous delight,
Now rapture rose to hear each cry.
We ventured out into the evening light.

We gasped for air and fought the night,
Not wanting to let go of this strong embrace.
The stars shared our hearts, shining bright.

And now in completion of our lover's rights,
Passions subsided to a simmer until, when next,
We'd venture out into the evening light,
The stars sharing our hearts, shining bright.

This List Gets Shorter

At this time of year, you notice.
It's something you may not think about,
But over time it happens.

It's a shock when you realise it,
Doing the annual things to make sure
You don't miss anyone.

You start with the family first,
And then move on to friends.
But this year it was the family list
That made me stop in recognition.

A whole layer, a whole level,
A whole generation is not there.
The grief hits you again.
Your eyes fill.

The Christmas present list,
The Birthday present list.
You are missing from both of these now.
But I'll never stop missing you here...
Deep within my heart.

Missing our elders who have passed.

An Ode to Flapjack

Who am I to decide whether you live or die?
Who am I to choose when it's your time?
And yet this burden like a weight, hangs around my neck,
As I stand here, asked your fate to decide.

Forgive me. What is the choice?
Allow you to stay as you are,
Until your little heart can beat no more?
And in that time what pain might you suffer and endure?
Should I care or should I bother?

You cannot tell in words of man,
Even though I stretch out my hand and touch your fur,
And hear your gentle purr,
As you try to reduce my stress
To this decision I must face.

Do you know the meaning of these words,
We say above your head?
Who am I to make this choice, to dim
The spark of life within your tiny body.

I would see your life expand and never die.
But there are more things in place of death.
Like pain and suffering, grief and distress.
My love for you would wish to see for you more than this.

As I know that life beyond exists. And it does.
Your little light will persist in another place and time.
Maybe as another Cat to grace another soul with love,
And with that, you would bring them joyful bliss.
So much from one so small.
Chasing ribbon, wool and feathers,
 Birds, mice and anything at all that might catch your fancy.

But curling up on someone's chest,
Or sitting in a warm lap,
That might suit you best.

Did you know as you turned to great each of us,
Standing around to bid you farewell?
Long will your memory linger in my heart,
And the joy and beauty of your life fill my thoughts -
As continues to be the case for each little life-light
That has shared this journey with me over my lifetime.

So, I decided to do what I can to ease the pain of your final days.
I bear the pain of knowing that I might indeed be shortening those days,
In the belief that in doing so, you will no longer suffer.

What a gruesome choice to have to make,
Each time a faithful friends and companion
Stands before this gate.
I have been here before.
And it gets no easier.

Forgive me!
Thank you for the life you chose to share with me.
Beautiful little Flapjack,
Eater of Bumble Bees.

And I Miss You

All of a sudden I miss you.
I hear someone speak with an accent just like yours.
And you travel straight into my mind,
Down into the heart of me and
It brings back memories of how we used to pass the time.

There you go. Your voice, and speaking again,
Talking at my innermost being.
And I miss you.
Deeper than I ever thought I would.
Stronger than I thought possible, is my heart full of yearning.
And I should not.
But... I miss you.

The strength of your arms around me.
The funny things you'd always say.
There was always something you managed to make me laugh about every day.

I can see your smile.
Always more like a smirk.
As if you couldn't allow yourself to break open
That heart that was always so delicate.

And it only seems like yesterday,
When you and your love, which kept me whole,
Melted and faded away.

And I miss you.

Life Is...

Life is in all its glory supreme,
Displayed as a gentle breeze,
Or burning lava flow.

Life is...

The tweeting bird at morning's call.
The galloping herds across the field.
Life is in all its glory supreme.

What is its power cannot be seen,
Neither what makes the growing leaf.
Or burning lava flow.

Life is...

As droplets fall from suspended air,
Gushing thunderously down mountain streams.
Life is in all its glory supreme.

We find she has created all we see,
Even galaxies and universal legacies,
Or burning lava flow.

Life...

She cannot be questioned
Or halted in her march of creation.
Life is in all its glory supreme,
Like burning lava flow.

Life is...

I'm A Poet

Tonight, I'm a poet,
At times, not knowing how it perfuses through my soul
And my entire being
Just to project the trueness of who I am and how I feel.

Tonight, I'll take you with me,
Through the meandering woods of my mind,
My emotions, the physicality that makes me, me.

Yes, tonight, I'm a poet.
The truth is I've always known it,
But mostly put it aside, to ride the platforms of what we're told we must be to succeed.
This has only led to miseries.

Tonight, I stand up. Tonight, I stand here
And boldly declare,
I am a poet and yes, I know it.
And in all of my irreverence to tradition
And what scholars insist a poet or poetry should be,
Tonight, tomorrow, and every day, this, is me.
I am a poet, and being a poet sets me free.

Poetic Place

You have the poetic judges,
Who listen through a microscope.
Then you have those who are just out
To have some fun and a joke.

There are those who spend their time,
Judging the tempo, the rhythms, and the rhyme.
Some others are not so fussed with that.
It's all about releasing the muse from the mind.

Whichever camp you sit in, there is a place for you.
Pull up a large rock-stone or drag a wooden stool.
It's the energy, the creativity, whatever topic you choose,
Whichever way you decide to let your word-paintings loose.

I'm not bothered with metre or the drastic need to rhyme.
I prefer to be taken away to another place and time.
For me it's the impression that you leave,
How you affect my mind and make my emotions feel,
Time after time.

Did I get your true idea?
Was the topic made clear?
Do the words you choose leave butterflies in my ears?

If your words have made me feel
As though I need to grab my pen and start to write.
Then you're my kind of poet.
I'm glad I heard your words tonight.

Don't let the poetic judgers dissuade you from wanting to write.
Don't feel discouraged by the poetic judging types.
They have their place, a world where others like them write.
A world where strict adherence to meter,
And words that no one knows, is their foresight.

There are other poetic places.
Worlds of less strict distinctions.
Lightness, with openness to wider poetic contradictions.

Word creativity is a mosaic.
A jigsaw puzzle of a kind with sharp, straight and rounded edges
That find their place over time.

Now overlaying these many pieces and shapes
The most beautiful picture is placed.
If we can only see with our hearts
The love for story and words
That all poetry displays.

About the Author

Sandra Pollock OBE MA

Sandra was born in the UK of Barbadian heritage. She has always written poetry and songs, and created art. She loves abstract art - probably, she says, because she is not often patient enough to create more life-like work.

Sandra has a passion for encouraging women from African, Caribbean and Asian communities to write their stories and experiences. She runs several creative writing workshops throughout the year, along with an annual Women's Poetry Competition in her local area.

Sandra is an entrepreneur, Founder of SHINE Together CIC, The Women's Awards, Open Mind Training & Development Ltd, Inspiring You CIC. She currently holds a number of NED roles and has chaired various regional and national organisations.

Her work on equality has seen her speak at the EU Committee on issues of flexible working, equality in the workplace and the benefits of getting women back into work. She has conducted many local, regional, and national business growth and other projects across England, Scotland, and Wales. In particular, she had worked to engage with under-represented groups in the workplace and the community.

Sandra is also an international speaker, author, and Consultant on Leadership, Management, Organisational Change, Inclusion and Diversity, working with senior leaders to recognise and incorporate the benefits of difference and create equality within organisations.

Sandra was awarded the Order of the British Empire (OBE) for services to Equality in the late Queen Elizabeth II's New Year's Honours List in December 2020.

Sandra holds a Master of Arts in Creative Writing from the University of Leicester, along with several other professional qualifications and awards gained over her many years of community and corporate work.

SanRoo Publishing

To find out more about SanRoo Publishing
visit our website at:

www.sanroopublishing.co.uk

Follow us on Facebook: @SanRooPublishing

or Twitter: @SanRooWriters

SanRoo Publising
is a Division of Inspiring You C.I.C.
26 Bramble Way, Leicester, LE3 2GY, UK.

Registered in England. Company No.: 10213814

www.ingramcontent.com/pod-product-compliance
Lightning Source LLC
Chambersburg PA
CBHW041313110526
44591CB00022B/2902